Deep Roots, Wide Branches

Deep Roots, Wide Branches

Poetry for Everyone

by

Jenni Wyn Hyatt

Cover illustration by Cathy Knight

In memory of my parents,
Edgar and Jennie, with
thanks for walks up the
'Urlin' and a happy childhood.

Diolch o galon.

Jenni Wyn Hyatt, née Williams, was born in Maesteg in 1942. She is married to Pete Hyatt and now lives in Derbyshire. In this, her third collection, she writes about family and friends, gardens and nature, subjects dear to her heart. Water features prominently, since how can plants grow without water? The collection branches out to include poems about places, poverty, injustice and the 'elusive muse'.

Many of the poems are written in free verse but you will also find here a variety of poetic forms. Fellow poets will, no doubt, be familiar with haiku, senryu, tanka, sonnet, villanelle, huitain, haibun, triolet, cinquain, dizain and rondeau, all of which feature in this collection, but it matters not if such terms are a mystery to you. This is accessible poetry, easy to understand on a first or second reading.

Contents

Family and Friends

The Garden and Nature

Places

Reaching Out

That Elusive Muse

Acknowledgments

Family
and
Friends

Echoes

dead fifty-eight years
Dad still holds my hand – I strive
to match his stride

For my father, Edgar Williams, 1905 - 1965

old photographs -
half forgotten voices
echo down the years

Balancing Act

I still see you now, standing behind the
counter
in your shop coat, with your eye on the
scales,
deducting a copper or two from the price
for the poor, regaining it from the rich.

I can still see the columns of figures
so neat and accurate in your ledger,
your unfailing grasp, not only of numbers,
but of economics and politics, far
exceeding mine. You were not much older
starting work as a delivery boy
than I was going to the Grammar School.
I try to imagine you, your face pale
under your flat cap, your frail body
battling with the bicycle's heavy frame.

After university I became
a teacher; you both thought it would be
easier
than the life of a nurse or a small town
grocer.
My ledgers were mark books, attendance
registers,
the many pointless records governments
demanded,
my customers often recalcitrant.

As time went on I found my satisfaction
in helping students who were disadvantaged
to realise potential they scarcely knew they
had -
trying, just like you, Dad, to balance the
scales.

For my father, Edgar Williams, 1905 - 1965

A Nurse's Anecdotes

I always knew
she'd had another life,
pre-motherhood.
I loved listening to her tales.

She told of tottering to interviews
on stiletto heels
because she wasn't the regulation
minimum height.

She spoke
of the five-year-old boy,
dying of lung cancer,
who called her
'the nurse with the smiley face' -
his dad a sixty a day smoker.

She recounted the time
a dog ran out
in front of her bicycle,
how she fell
and all her medical instruments
smashed;
how she persuaded
those in power
to provide taxis

for the midwives at night,
Portsmouth being a dangerous place
for young ladies on bikes.

Then there was the time
she defied the consultant
to save a baby
who'd been born not breathing
and all the occasions
when various doctors
asked for her help with diagnoses.

Admiring such skill,
it's no wonder
I wanted to be a nurse...
but it was not to be.

*Remembering my mother, Jennie, née
Evans, 1910 – 1971*

The Smile

I have a photograph of my mother,
aged about twelve, with her two brothers,
wearing a long-sleeved dress
she'd knitted herself - and smiling
her inimitable smile.
She told me she'd had to wear that dress
in the absence of anything more suitable
for a Sunday school trip to the seaside
on a sweltering hot day.
I'll bet she never complained,
never stopped smiling.

There's a photograph of her
that my father used to keep
in his wallet. She's wearing
a print summer dress
and smiling at the camera,
so slim then,
hair fashionably waved,,
thirties style.

For their wedding she wore
a powder-blue suit
and the most glorious hat,
rose-budded and netted,
kept for years in a proper hat box,
on top of the wardrobe,
still full of trapped confetti.
She smiled
a little shyly that day.

In my favourite photograph
she sits on a hospital windowsill,
black-stockinged,
her nurse's uniform suiting her so well,
the pristine apron,
the starched cap, that smile
radiating confidence and efficiency.

Even just before she died,
far too young, at sixty-one,
she tried to give us
one last, tremulous smile.

*For my mother, Jennie, née Evans, 1910 –
1971*

Grampi Annwyl

Grampi annwyl,
champion of the young,
defending us always
against the sharp tongues
of mother and grandmother.

Born on a smallholding
in a Cardiganshire village,
you became a plasterer,
moved to the valleys,
helped build the chapel,
where you taught in adult Sunday school,
and were a stalwart
of the weekly prayer meetings.
Welsh your first language,
you never mastered how to say
'wood' and 'wool' the English way.
They were always 'ood' and 'ool',
Grampi annwyl.

You worked until nearly seventy;
I remember plucking bits of plaster

from your work dungarees,
cutting your toenails,
when your back was too stiff to bend.
My older cousin and I used to sit in the shed
at the top of your immaculate garden
surrounded by sawdust,
wood shavings and gardening tools.
We both adored you,
Grampi annwyl.

Well into your eighties, you climbed ladders
to replace missing slates, inspect errant
chimneys.
It was rumoured that you
had a temper, swore at work.
I never heard it. To me you were
the epitome of all that was good, kind and
gentle.
I love you still, Grampi annwyl.

annwyl - dear

*In memory of my maternal grandfather, Rhys
Evans, 1880 – 1976*

Gran Caerau

Born in poverty on Ynys Môn,
the eldest of nine, she had no shoes
so could not go to school.
Knowing the 23rd Psalm by heart,
she taught herself to read,
tallying the letters to the sounds.
She married, moved south,
where there was work in the mines
for my grandfather,
found her *Noddfa* in chapel,
gained the community's respect.

She lost her eldest,
a fifteen-year-old son, to pneumonia
and a nine-year-old daughter to peritonitis
in the same year,
before the discovery of penicillin,
my father, born after their deaths,
much cherished.

My memory of her is hazy;
she died when I was two - but
I know that she sewed.
I had her old Singer machine,
made curtains, clothes,
turned many a collar and cuff -

until a part wore out
and could not be replaced.
I have her treadle table still.

She revelled in pretty things;
her china tea set,,
orange, indigo and gold
has been on display
in all my homes,
treasured, kept clean,
gazed at every day.
I have a photograph that testifies
to her fondness for jewellery.
Having so much in common,
I like to think
we might have been close.

The meaning of 'Noddfa' is 'sanctuary'.

*'Gran Caerau', Margaret, known as 'Marged',
Williams née Jones (1865 – 1945) was my
paternal grandmother. She spent most of her
adult life in Caerau, the topmost part of the
Llynfi Valley, where she attended Noddfa
Baptist Chapel, now a community centre.*

Recurring Dream

I try to ring them almost every night;
the need to speak to them gets more
compelling.
I can't get through; the number is not right.

I find myself in such a piteous plight;
I don't know what's gone wrong – there is no
telling.
I try to ring them almost every night.

I fail repeatedly, try as I might,
tsunami-like, my panic keeps on swelling.
I can't get through; the number is not right.

Although I won't give up without a fight,
close to the surface now, the tears are
welling.
I try to ring them almost every night.

Has someone changed the code, just out of
spite?
I'm frantic now; I'm getting close to yelling.
I can't get through; the number is not right.

Much in my mind, though distant from my
sight;
when we will meet again there's no
foretelling.

I try to ring them almost every night
but only Heaven knows which number's
right.

*This is a real recurring dream that I had
decades after both my parents were dead. I
was trying to ring them using their old phone
number but failing to get through. No
combination I tried was successful, and I
used to wake up in a panic.*

Anti Nel's Bara Brith

Scribbled in an old notebook,
Anti Nel's bara brith recipe,
'Mwged o fflwr a mwged o laeth,
mwged o hyn a mwged o'r llall',
a mug of flour, a mug of milk,
a mug of this and a mug of that –
a medley of dried fruit,
currants, raisins, glacé cherries
'neu beth bynnag's 'da ti' -
or whatever you've got.
I can hear her voice now, picture her
as she listed the ingredients,
explained the method.

She 'went into service' at thirteen,
married a Methodist minister,
bore two daughters..
Diminutive, she lacked
neither brains nor style,
had her own opinions
on politics and world affairs,
championed the weak,
the poor, the oppressed,
epitomised Welsh hospitality,
radiated kindness and compassion.
Every time I use the recipe, I think of her.

More cake than bread,
it's speckled, through and through,
with her love for me
and mine for her.

*Bara brith, 'speckled bread', is a Welsh
speciality, served sliced with butter.*

*'Anti Nel' (Eleanor Evans, 1917 – 2010) was
my mother's first cousin.*

William John

A farmer's son,
what did he know of war?
A sniper's gun,
a grave far away from home,
a plaque on the chapel wall.

*In memory of my mother's cousin, William
John Evans, of Plasnewydd, Penuwch (1920
– 1944) a brother to Anti Nel. He is buried in
Ranville War Cemetery, grave number
IV.F.12. His grave has been visited often by
family members. It is my hope that future
generations will continue to honour him.*

*This is the 'englyn' on Penuwch Chapel wall,
also commemorating another young soldier:*

*William John dinam a Daniel – pwy nawr
Ond Penuwch gai'u harddel
A'u rhifo'n meddau rhyfel
Don't eto'n rhydd, ddydd a ddêl.*

*Faultless William John and Daniel,
who now but Penuwch will claim them
and count them amongst the graves of war?
The day will come when they will be free
again.*

Annie's Story

They'd sent the postcard
in 1916,
soon after their marriage.
I saw, in sepia and white,
the fields and hills of Cardiganshire,
the footsteps of my ancestors
imprinted there. I heard 'iaith y nefoedd',
the language of heaven,
on their tongues,
smelled the clean air,
the sweet breath
of dog roses and docile cattle,
the scent of hay.
I imagined the young couple's
hopes and dreams.

They'd met in London, I believe,
Annie in service there,
a quarry worker's daughter,
from the Rhondda,
Evan a tailor's assistant.
They'd made their home
in his village
in rural West Wales.
Did she miss her friends,
the hustle and bustle

of London, or of valley life?

I'll never know. Married barely a year,
Evan succumbed -
to tuberculosis.
Annie returned to the Rhondda…

I never discovered
the end of her story.

Evan David Thomas, who died on July 25th
1917, aged 29, was my maternal
grandmother's brother. He is buried in
Penuwch Chapel Cemetery, Ceredigion, as
is his mother, great grandmother Jane, who
died in 1901, also of tuberculosis, aged 42.

That Little Girl

That little girl
plays footsie with her father
under the table,
holding his hand -
and trying to eat.

That little girl
curls up on the horsehair settee
reading 'Sunny Stories'
as the clock chimes
from the top of the sideboard.

That little girl
tends her flower garden;
a little older, she helps in the shop,
attends chapel with her Dad
on Sunday evenings.

That little girl,
an old woman now,
still grieves for the father
who died
when she was twenty-two.

The sideboard smiles
from another wall
and the clock,
erratic now
chimes on.

The Hurling Fields

Summer evening walks
up 'the Urlin'
with our parents,
the gold and purple of buttercups and
foxgloves,
bold ox-eye daisies,
the scent of honeysuckle and dog roses,
the plaintive call of a peewit.

Up we'd trek to the grassy sward
guarded by the oak tree we used to climb,
bounded by the brook where we paddled.
I can picture it now, playing cricket,
Dad teaching us how to hold the bat
and bowl overarm,
Mam lying on the grass,
pretty in her print summer frock,
watching.

Decades later my brother and I
went and searched for the spot
to no avail.
Erased by time, nature and humankind,
the picture exists now
only in our minds.

Two Childhood Haiku

a puddle
a pair of wellies
paradise

when there's a stone bridge
a gurgling brook - and pooh sticks
we are all children

For all our children, grandchildren and future generations

The Last One

We'd never been just a couple,
the children were there from the start
in various combinations;
we were always a family.
When the older ones began to leave
one by one, it felt normal, natural,
like winter after autumn or Monday
after the weekend.

But when the youngest moved away,
I struggled to adapt,
crumbled, flaky as pastry;
unwonted tears welling like water
from a hidden spring,
teetering like a vertiginous walker
on a cliff edge,
fearing to fall
and dash myself
to pieces
on the rocks
below.

The Giggles

Long ago in chapel,
clothed in our Sunday best
and Welsh nonconformist respectability,
our grandfather sitting in the 'Big Seat'
below the pulpit,
my youngest cousin and I sat
in the family pew,
next to our grandmother.

Something tickled us.
Whether it was a phrase
the pious preacher uttered
or a feather
in someone's Sunday hat
I no longer know -
but we started to giggle
and could not stop.

Scandalised, my grandmother dug me in the ribs
with her sharp elbow.
I passed the dig to my cousin.
We stuffed handkerchiefs into our mouths,
desperately tried to control ourselves,
but it was too late.
Overwhelmed by laughter,
we abandoned our souls to the devil.

The Age of Steam

How I miss
the screech of the whistle,
the hiss
of steam at the station,
the belch of smoke,
the click-clack of the track,
even the soot.

How I miss
the corridor,
the proper compartments,
the engines, Earls, Kings and Castles,
the little notebook
in which I recorded their names,
long lost.

How I wish
I could see again
that childhood handwriting,
re-live those journeys,
stop at Adlestrop,
ponder the empty platform,
listen to the birds.

*This poem recalls stopping at Adlestrop on a
train journey to stay with relatives and
sharing the feelings Edward Thomas
expressed in his famous poem.*

Jessie

Sectioned, committed, safely locked away
when just a girl, considered mad, insane;
mentioned in whispers, gossip kept at bay,
a stigma, a respected household's shame.

What happened to you in the infancy
of treatment? Did they mutilate your brain,
seizures induced, a botched lobotomy
ensuring you could not be free again?

What did you dream of, Jess, before the
curse
of mental illness ravaged all you'd known?
Might you have been a teacher or a nurse,
got married and borne children of your own?

We'll never know what might have been your
choice,
sequestered as you were, denied a voice.

Jessie Sydonia Heloise Nash (1909 – 1994)
was a relative by marriage, great aunt to my
two older children. She died in a mental
health institution aged eighty-four, having
spent almost her entire life locked away. The
official diagnosis, apparently, was
schizophrenia, but, knowing the family

history, I suspect that Jessie may have been severely autistic.

Some of the ideas in this sonnet came from researching early treatments for schizophrenia.

Before

Before
the blessings and betrayals,
the desires and divorces,
the children and the childlessness,
the plenty and the poverty,
four sixteen-year-old girls
in regulation striped dresses
skipped school
one summer afternoon.

In a little-known valley
by a stone bridge
they dreamed their dreams,
dabbled hands and feet
in a mountain stream
and, long before
the digital age
a Brownie box camera
recorded, in black and white,
that hallowed water,
that carefree day.

Cats

They bring delightful presents of dead mice;
they'll stalk them patiently then pounce and
slay –
apart from that they're really rather nice.

If you are feeling ill they'll sacrifice
their fun and lie beside you all the day -
or bring delightful presents of dead mice.

I must admit they have another vice –
refusing food they *gobbled* yesterday!
Apart from that they're really rather nice.

An evening on your lap is paradise
except for the occasional foray
to bring delightful presents of dead mice.

They'll devastate your carpets in a trice
by scratching. When you sleep they want to
play.
Apart from that they're really rather nice.

I'll give you one last snippet of advice –
A cat will rarely let you have *your* way.
despite delightful presents of dead mice
I still maintain they're really rather nice!

Ernie

We called him Fiddle-Faddle,
my darling Ernie,
for nothing was safe
from his prying paws,
and sharp little teeth.
His eyes were wide and green
in a guileless face
that seemed forever smiling.
He had a black spot
beneath his white chin
like a goatee beard
and jigsaw curves of white
behind his black ears.
He adored digestive biscuits,
gave kisses on demand,
loved to be held
like a teddy bear
up in my arms.
When I was ill in bed
he never left me,
guarded me all day,
looking concerned.

Part cat, part dog,
part human,
he understood
every word I said,
or so I thought.
He had far too few
of his nine lives,
killed on the road,
aged only two,
but, in those two short years,
he gave and received
vast quantities of love.
Over thirty years later,
his portrait still hangs
by my bed.

In memory of Ernie, 1990 to 1992.

Mabon

Handsome in black and white,
evening-suited night-time rambler,
bright-eyed you wave
your banner of a tail.
Mouse-catcher, bird-watcher,
gruesome-gift-bearer,
muddy-footprint-maker,
biscuit-cruncher,
smoked-salmon-gobbler,
your purrful midnight cuddles never fail
to make me smile,
belovéd Mabon mine.

Mabon, 2007 to 2023

*Mabon was very much alive when this poem
was written but became ill and had to be 'put
to sleep' just before the book was published.
The house feels very empty.*

Dreaming

Sometimes
a dream is all
it takes to conjure up
your face around the bedroom door -
Mabon.

One night
you jumped up on
the bed and afterwards
you ran outside and climbed a tree -
run free.

Visit
when you can, come,
purr in my ear. Until
next time I'll hold you in my heart -
always.

The Garden and Nature

Garden Villanelle

I watch my garden changing every day,
a palette of delight for aging eyes.
"Let's take a turn round our estate," we say,

although, in truth, it's just a little way –
it's only half a tennis court in size,
I watch my garden changing every day.

Each season has its own unique display;
I love it just the same in every guise.
"Let's take a turn round our estate," we say.

Hawthorn intoxicates in early May
and all the singing birds extemporise.
I watch my garden changing every day.

We barbecue in summer sun's last rays
and still sit on and see the slow moon rise.
"Let's take a turn round our estate," we say.

It's been hard work – the soil is solid clay –
but we've created quite a paradise.

I watch my garden changing every day;
"Let's take a turn round our estate," we say.

Starlings

You small-time gangsters, oh you tapestry
of lustrous emerald and purple threads,
a cloud from nowhere, veiled in mystery,
a swarm of locusts on my flower beds.

Bold knights in armour, braggadocious
leaders,
how glamorous your rabble, stylish mob,
you draw your swords and decimate my
feeders,
how clamorous your babble, rowdy yobs.

A raucous rooftop choir, brashly singing,
an ambulance whose strident siren wails,
a telephone that rings, an oven pinging;
your clever imitation rarely fails.

Incorrigible copycats, such mimics,
indulge me - what will be tomorrow's
gimmicks?

View from the Top

Perched high at the top of our garden,
we listen to the thrush's jubilation
and, drenched in the scent of lilac and
bluebells,
we gaze down over the town,
past the dome of the Old Chemistry Lab,
a miniature St Paul's,
over the burnished rooftops
to Old College, that mock Gothic storehouse
of youthful memories - to the castle
and the glorious war memorial,
its womanly form like a ship's proud
figurehead,
baring her bosom to the waves.
With her, we watch, until the sun begins to
set
over Cardigan Bay.

*The view from the top of the garden in the
house in Aberystwyth where we lived from
January 2006 until December 2014*

Spring Haibun

Robins, breasts aflame, string together their
sweet cadences like ropes of pearl. The first
skylarks of the year spiral up and away,
trailing crystal droplets of song in their wake.
On the lake, mallards' heads gleam with a
sheen of emerald, while courting grebes
proudly display their amber cravats.

on a short spring walk
nature flaunts her dowry
of vibrant jewels

Sonnet in June

Dog roses, petals soft as babies' skin,
adorn the hedgerows; fledglings leave their
nests
while hirundines catch insects on the wing
and baby robins bare their speckled breasts.

Brimful with nectar, bold red campions draw
prospecting insects to their vivid blooms.
Regal in purple, foxglove spires soar
while honeysuckle shares its sweet perfume.

Each ox-eye daisy turns its smiling face
towards the sun; the cuckoo calls in flight.
The elder flaunts its flowers of fragrant lace,
and fields of golden buttercups delight.

How often will we see so rich a June
if urgent action is not taken soon?

*Hirundines: swallows, sand martins and
house martins*

Summer Evening

We sit and watch the summer moon's slow
climb,
drink in the honeysuckle's heady scent.
Relaxed and quite oblivious of the time
we sit and watch the summer moon's slow
climb,
an evening occupation so sublime.
The barbecue sinks low, its warmth all spent
-
but still we watch the summer moon's slow
climb,
drink in the honeysuckle's heady scent.

Two Bird Haiku

swallows leave again
flying over furrowed fields
my wrinkles deepen

treetops stir
beneath the stars
an owl hoots

An Uphill Walk

the mew

of a buzzard

the shriek

of a jay

the wind

in the trees

the steepness

of the hill

the tap

of her white stick

Two Late Summer Haiku

blackberries
the hedgerow's
caviar

stillness in the air
top-heaviness in the trees
late summer torpor

A Touch of Autumn in August

I reach
for the sweetness
of blackberries – a faint
whisper of gossamer brushes
my wrist.

Putting the Garden to Bed

It's a long process
when you're aging and aching,
putting the garden to bed,
pruning and planting,
trimming the hedges,
sweeping the drifts of dead leaves,
first crisp, then soggy,
for the compost.

Doing a little each day,
we work, through the glory
of the titian leaves,
the purple splendour of the asters
and Michaelmas daisies,
to the gloom of early winter,
the garden dead and leafless -
but not lifeless...

For, in those final stages,
in the misery of the dark, bleak afternoons,

we see the spring bulbs rising,
early snowdrops shining
their tiny lamps
and just as I pluck
the last spindly rosebuds for the table,
I glimpse
the first Christmas rose.

Two Winter Haiku

winter evening meal
bright berries deck the table
candles burn with hope

frost holds earth hostage;
ice scribbles its signature
at the lake's edge

Highlight

Birdwatching
on wind-stirred dunes,
walking difficult,
birdlife scarce.
Leaning over the rail
of a viewing platform,
I meet the gentle eye
of a shy muntjac deer.
Startled, she takes flight,
bounds away.
I see the white
of her retreating tail,
the highlight
of an unrewarding day.

The Hermit (a little story)

We watched as he made his way, every morning and evening, down to the well near our home. Frail and thin, he made slow progress, picking his steps carefully, fearful of falling. His skin was as leathery as the water containers he carried, his hair as white as the old man's beard that adorns the hedges in late summer, his hands as gnarled as the bark of the oaks that clung precariously to the rocky slope.

We worried about him, my wife and I, living alone in that austere sandstone cave. He'd tried to make it cosy, with a straw pellet and rough blankets for a bed and a fire in winter, but he spent hours kneeling on his arthritic knees on the rocky floor, hands clasped together, muttering and gazing at a wooden cross he had nailed to the wall. It was a strange, lonely life.

Sometimes, in warm weather, we'd take the little ones up to see him. He seemed to love that - and sometimes, frugal as it was, he would share his meal with us. I used to sing to him, a different song for each season, and his face would light up with pleasure.

We care about human beings, we robins.

Places

Penmaenmawr Retreat

Scarred by their quarrying past, protective
hills
enfold you - and ahead the bright sea
gleams.
You hear a blackbird's song, a robin's trill,
the cry of gulls, the gurgle of a stream.

And if you venture up those gorse-lit slopes
you'll meet the ghosts of those who've gone
before,
stone circles formed by Neolithic folk,
the plane crash site, a tragedy of war.

Fair Môn, Mam Cymru, lies across the Strait.
Eryri's peaks are not too far away
while castles, waterfalls and walks await
and diverse beaches will enhance your
stay…

The quarries are all gone, tourism reigns,
a way of life is lost; the language wanes.

Eryri: Snowdonia
Môn, Mam Cymru: Anglesey, the Mother of
Wales

Aber Falls (near Bangor in North Wales)

Did the Bronze and Iron Age people
in their round houses
admire the beauty of Y Rhaeadr Fawr,
the big waterfall?
Did they give thanks
for the purity of the water,
worship its gods and goddesses,
show their gratitude with votive offerings?

Did Llywelyn the Great
ride here with his followers
from his court close by?
Did the hunting horn sound
over the Carneddau foothills?
Did the arrows fly,
bringing down hares and deer
for feasts in the great hall?
Were prayers for victory in battle
offered in the chapel to a Christian god?

Today we walk here for exercise, for
pleasure,
to watch the dippers and grey wagtails
flit from stone to stone
in the bright-eyed, laughing stream,
to marvel at the height of the cataract,
descending, powerful yet delicate,
like a long, white chiffon scarf
from the throat of the rock,
to feel the breeze-borne spray touching our
faces,
at one with earth, sky and water -
a modern spirituality.

The Nymphaeum (at Chedworth Roman Villa in Gloucestershire)

Written in the voice of a completely imaginary resident I think of as 'Jana'

It's so different,
here, near Corinium,
from our home in Amalfi,
where, from our villa's terraces
we stepped down to the sea
and the days were steeped in sunshine.

After a long, cold winter,
it's late spring now.
I've picked bluebells
to decorate the nymphaeum,
to give thanks to the Naiad
for the refreshing spring water
piped to supply the kitchen,
wash out the latrines,
give us the luxury of baths and steam.

Health-giving, gentle rain
makes colours softer here,
the vegetation green.
I wake to a chorus
of blackbirds and thrushes;
nightingales lull me to my dreams.

This is my home now.
If only I felt well!
I pray to Aesculapius
to rid me of the fog
that dulls my brain,
to heal me of this niggling, gnawing pain.

*Nymphaeum: a sanctum usually consecrated
to water nymphs
Corinium: Cirencester
Naiad: a nymph of rivers, lakes, springs and
fountains
Aesculpaius: Roman god of healing*

*Her illness, lead poisoning, is caused by the
pipes that carry the water.*

Seaside Companion

She was in charge
that November day.
Under her hand the wild horses
reared and lunged,
crested and plunged
frothing and foaming,
their manes glinting white
in the autumn sunshine.
She churned the dogs
into a frenzy of excitement,
so that they chased and cavorted,
around the beach.
Playfully she threw
handfuls of sand
into my eyes, splashed me
with drenching sea water.

On the dunes,
she started her tricks again,
holding me so that I could not move
or tossing me hither and thither,
so that I grasped, hopelessly,
at clumps of marram grass
and low brambles
to keep my balance,
stumbled into rabbit holes,
fell headlong
more than once.

Eventually,
I retreated

leaving the storm
to blow herself out.

(Storm Arwen, St Ives, November 2021)

A Favourite Place

The church spire
across the rippling water,
the morning walk
to the boulangerie,
the aroma
of freshly baked baguettes,
the kiss of sun on pale skin,
the quack of mallards,
the clang of bicycle bells,
the swoop of terns,
the stately heron
guarding the weir,
the rich taste of croissants,
the thrum of a day in waiting.

Evening brings
the barbecue's sizzle,
the soft hum of voices,
the walk along the riverside path,
the courtesy of greetings,
the croak of bullfrogs,
the nod of sunflowers,
once, an old, whiskered dog otter,
always, a 'kee, kee' and then the flash
of a kingfisher.

We meant to visit one last time,
then came the pandemic.
Age tightened its grip,
Savonnieres beside the Cher,
I never got the chance...

to say goodbye.

Monet's Garden in May

The layout's formal but the planting's wild
in Monet's garden - a delight to view,
scrambling and tumbling like a joyous child.
Huge bearded irises of every hue,
stand, mouths agape to drink the morning
dew,
and on the bridge of water-lily fame,
standing with Pete, our friend, John, lives
anew,
hand raised in greeting from a silver frame.

*In memory of John, 1951 – 2019. The
photograph stands on our sideboard.*

Baslow Edge, Derbyshire, late August

The mauvy-pink of heather mists the heath,
vast gritstone boulders guard the valley view.
Backlit, a plump cloud billows - and beneath,
a kestrel hovers dark against the blue.

Shy harebells flourish in the sheltered spots,
bracken exudes its bracing, earthy scent,
a pair of wheatears flickers on a rock,
a swallow banks and turns with sure intent.

Nothing escapes the Frog Stone's bulbous
gaze;
he's witnessed work and worship on this
moor,
seen countless generations walk these
ways;
the breeze we feel has passed this way
before.

Here lovers wander free – and many a
pledge
is whispered in the wind on Baslow Edge.

Reaching Out

I Light a Candle

I light a candle, watch the shadows sway,
recall disasters, see the scenes replay;
on anniversaries, to show I care,
denote respect for grief beyond repair,
it flickers in my window, marks the day.

In churches or cathedrals, when I pray
for all whose lives have somehow gone
astray,
for those brought low by sickness or
despair,
I light a candle.

When skies are ash and cloudbanks glower
grey,
when sleety showers lash the sullen air,
when days are short and darkness hard to
bear,
to nurture hope, to drive the gloom away,
I light a candle.

Poverty

Poverty,
I have lived with you,
felt your icy breath on my
scrawny neck,
stared deep
into your fish-cold eyes,
shivered under
your thin blankets.
I have worn
your cast-off clothes
and squeezed
my growing feet
into your too-tight shoes.

For years you have kept
your distance from me -
but now, once more,
I see you prowl
cheek by jowl with Austerity
stealing homes,

extinguishing hopes,
dispensing
your nefarious legacy,
of haggard faces,
hungry children.

While the rich get richer,
I smell your
noxious breath
and am ashamed.

Who are they?

Indifferent to anyone in need,
they seek their own advancement every day;
their stimuli are selfishness and greed.

Superiority's their central creed;
their attitudes quite clearly convey
indifference to anyone in need.

They care not for the planet – it can bleed
if they can make a profit on the way;
their stimuli are selfishness and greed.

Though many go to church, it's by their
deeds
that they'll be known – and, sadly, they
display
indifference to anyone in need.

Devoid of any scruples, they will feed
on others as do predators on prey.
Their stimuli are selfishness and greed.

A privileged and preferential breed,
their world is one where power and wealth
hold sway;
indifferent to anyone in need
their stimuli are selfishness and greed.

The Two Faces of Coal

A tragedy too painful to express -
the industry that was the valley's pride
shut down, a whole community's distress,
hard-working miners roughly cast aside
like outgrown toys, their livelihood denied.

This ancient vegetation we thought good,
that gives us heat and light and cooks our
food,
threatens our being. Science shows us how
it causes hurricanes and fire and flood.
Too late we've learned - *the tragedy is now.*

Storm Babet, October 2023

The wind buffets and wails,
shrieks and howls,
impales wet leaves
to window panes.
Lifted by its powerful hand
the empty dustbin bowls
down the alleyway,
clatters as the gale batters
our walls. Darkness assails
the windows. Relentless, rain falls.
Fearful, we stay inside,
reach for crosswords, books,
grateful for warm homes…

and that the wind's screech
is not the rocket's whine.

That Elusive Muse

Sometimes

Sometimes, when I am visiting a place,
I know that there's a poem waiting there,
as if it's simply hanging in the air –
and then the words will tumble out apace,
each elbowing and jostling for a space.
with images and cadences to spare.
At such times I know nothing of despair
and failure dare not show its surly face.
My muse can be a flower or a tree,
a sunset or a skein of geese in flight,
a fragile leaf that's only just unfurled,
the power of the vast, unfeeling sea,
soft whispers in the silence of the night
or sorrow for the sadness of the world.

What Happens to the Words?

What happens to the words? Sometimes
they fly
towards the stars and rocket to the moon.
Sometimes, earthbound, they wither and
they die.

Like birds ascending to a sunlit sky,
like buzzing bees who flit from bloom to
bloom,
what happens to the words? Sometimes they
fly.

Like careful preparations gone awry,
like hapless minstrels who forget their tune,
sometimes, earthbound, they wither and they
die.

As welcome as the curlew's bubbling cry,
the froth of foam, the softly floating spume -
the happiness of words that sometimes fly.

Like stagnant water, motionless, they lie,
like garden plants grown spindly in the
gloom,
sometimes, earthbound, they wither and they
die.

Like mountain hares who hear the breezes
sigh,
like patients fading in an airless room,
what happens to the words? Sometimes they
fly;
sometimes, earthbound, they wither and they
die.

Full Moon

Full moon tonight so will it stir
my moody, inconsistent muse
to action? Does she even care?
Full moon tonight so will it stir
imagination, be a spur
for poetry, ignite the fuse?
Full moon tonight so will it stir
my moody, inconsistent muse?

The Old Bard's Farewell

Once lithe and strong I strode from court to
court
and entertained the high-born with my
words,
assured of a welcome in their halls,
the warmth of fire, a cup of mead, good
food.

My sharp eyes spied shy snowdrops in the
woods,
pale ladies' smock along the river banks,
a silver fin that quivered in a stream,
a tiny goldcrest hiding in a bush.
Then verse was wont to bubble from my
throat
as freely as the tumbling waterfall.

My muse, elusive now, waxes and wanes;
it's left to younger bards to entertain
the gentry. Though their songs seem
passing strange
to my old ears, life and our art move on.

I did not hear the cuckoo call last spring,
a sign I shall not see another year.
I whisper at this Lammas-tide a prayer
that if this wintertime the Reaper comes,

he'll take me soft and swift, perchance at night
ere mind, sight, muse and memory are gone.

Atgo /
Remembrance
by Hedd Wyn

My Williams grandparents, from
Ynys Môn and my Evans
grandparents, from Ceredigion,
all spoke Welsh as their first
language. Some of them almost
certainly endured the indignity of
the infamous 'Welsh Not' at
school.

I include, in their honour, one of
my favourite poems by Hedd
Wyn and my translation of it.

Atgo

Dim ond y lleuad borffor
Ar fin y mynydd llwm
A sŵn hen Afon Prysor
Yn canu yn y cwm.

Hedd Wyn, Ellis Humphrey Evans, 1887 - 1917

Remembrance

Only the purple moonlight
on the barren hill,
old River Prysor singing
In the valley still.

First published in the book 'The Hero' by Michael Dante, 2022

Acknowledgements

Thanks to the editors of the following anthologies, journals, podcasts and websites who first published many of the poems included here:

Aberystwyth EGO, Dreich, Fresh Out Magazine, Good Dadhood, Literary Revelations, Manx Reflections, Paper Swans Press, Pause for Paws, Poetry Pea, Spelt Advent Calendar, The Lyric, The Poetry Kit, The Road Not Taken: a Journal of Formal Poetry, WestWard Quarterly.

Immeasurable thanks to my daughter, Cathy Knight, for the beautiful cover design and to my son-in-law, Tim Fox, for his technical expertise.

Thanks to Jim Bennett of 'The Poetry Kit' and to Wendy Pratt, on whose online courses some of these poems were written.

Thanks to the friends and family members who support my efforts.

Printed in Great Britain
by Amazon

43635661R00066